A Brave Lament

For Those Who Know Death

ANDREW & CHRISTY BAUMAN

In dedication to our son Jackson Brave Bauman

Contents

Andrew's entries will be marked with a tree icon

Christy's entries will be marked with a feather icon

ACKNOWLEDGMENTS

So many people made this book happen. First we'd like to thank our friends and our family who not only helped us raise money for the film and this book, but have carried us through this tragedy and have made it possible for us to birth a project like this. Your presence and your gifts have made this wild dream come to fruition. To our editor Traci Mullins, you were a God send. These pages are so painful and you took on our story with great wisdom and care. You helped craft this book into something gloriously raw in its beauty. Thank you. To our copy editor Rose Jackson, we thank you for your thoughtful engagement with this text, your tears and your deep belief and encouragement in this journey.

TO OUR BRAVE READER

Most likely you have picked up this book because you feel like a stranger in your grief, an alien visiting another planet. You stand outside of your own body watching your life from afar. Struck by tragedy, you may no longer feel like existing. This book is meant to accompany you during your season of despair.

This is not an easy read—not something you will necessarily enjoy. It may seem odd that we offer a book that invites you into our tragedy while you are navigating your own, but we would suggest that it is exactly what you need. Running away from pain or ignoring its existence doesn't make it go away; rather, it changes forms. Unaddressed tragedy becomes addiction, numbness, over-spiritualizing, or artificial placidity. When we run from our deepest pain, it will define us in ways we never imagined. We must have the courage to turn toward the tragedy and face the depths of our desolation.

The pages ahead are meant to give you the strength and support you need to bear the full weight of your loss. This a raw and sincere account of our first year of survival after losing our child, Jackson Brave Bauman, to a horrific cord accident the day before he was to be born. Nothing could have prepared us for what was to come.

In our search for Christian material on grief, we found limited resources to accompany us on this bitter journey. The only book we could stomach was Nicholas

Wolterstorff's *Lament for a Son*. His account of losing his own son was raw and transparent. He was honest about his deep questioning of God and faith, his ferocious love and terrible grief. All of the other material we found or were given felt inadequate. It wasn't as if the grief shared wasn't real, but it felt too polished and clean, and we didn't trust it.

Our grief was a dirty, cursing lament, a grief fraught with so much pain and rage that we couldn't bear one more "testimony" in which everything turned out awesome because of Jesus. We needed the author's blood on the pages. We needed a Jesus who was just as brokenhearted as we were, not some cosmic jerk who caused or allowed the death of our son. We could not believe in a cruel or passive God when God was all we had left.

We immediately suspended our private counseling practices, knowing we couldn't offer care to our clients unless we were willing to care for ourselves. With few resources, we set out on a pilgrimage of mourning, not having a clue where it would take us. A couple of months into our grief journey we traveled through Asia for months of writing, grieving, and trying to make sense of the senseless. We hope our expressions of grief can help you navigate your own. We don't think grief is bad, scary, or unholy. Raw lamentation is one of the most courageous and divine acts that God invites us into.

It has taken us six years since our traumatic loss to publicly tell our story. This year we produced a film and finally compiled our writings into the book you are holding now. We chose to make our film more neutral than faith-based so that more people would be able to relate to our story and receive comfort, even if they did not share our Christian beliefs. This book, however, depicts a wrestling match with our faith.

It offers an intimate look at our inner war to hold onto a good God in the midst of profound heartache. Please note that we designated each entry with a personal icon, to help the reader know who is writing. Christy's entries will be marked with a feather, and Andrew's writings with a tree. May you find solace here. May you find glimmers of hope and resurrection in the midst of your loss. May you too have the strength and courage to enter A Brave Lament.

-Andrew & Christy

Six months before our son's due date...

Dear Jackson Brave Bauman,

I can't wait to meet you. I have dreamed of what you will look like, act like, and what type of man you will become. You have been growing in your mother's womb for about six-and-a-half months now; I'll bet it's nice in there. You are expected to enter this world sometime around November 30th. I wanted to write and you tell you a few things as you anticipate entering this scary, glorious world of ours.

I must admit, I am terrified to raise you. I am trying to work through the pain of my story around your grandfather, my father, who was not around very much when I was a kid. This will inevitably impact you. I have fought so hard to allow myself to be fathered by others,

4

to father myself, and to allow our God to heal those infant places in my soul.

Much has been healed, but many tender scars remain.

Growing up feeling orphaned, I tried to blaze my own path. This path took many dark and unaccompanied turns. Loneliness and fear drove me to brokenness, deep heartache, and betrayal of myself and many I was in relationship with. Because of this, I fear for your journey too. I already feel my propensity to guard you, to try to protect you from this fallen world, to not let you be free to find your way. Yet none of us can escape evil's reach. You will be hurt. You will be betrayed by those you love the most. But my grasp for control over your life only reminds me that I am called to open my hands wider, to trust a God I often wrestle to believe in.

I want to assure you that in the midst of the inevitable pain you will experience in this world, you are deeply loved and covered. No matter what you choose, where you go, what you do, or how much you shatter my heart, you are madly and unconditionally loved. I will hold you lightly, my son, if you need to leave, to explore your world and the deep crevasses of your soul. I will let you go, but my arms and home will always be yours when you choose to return.

About your name… Your name holds much honor and legacy. "Jackson" is after your mother's grandparents, Mema & Awpa. They are stunning people. Their love and depth of spirit is a wonder to behold. Your mother's life was saved by their love, and it is a monumental reason why she is the light she is today.

"Brave" is a name I have held close to my heart for nearly a decade. I feel like it was a new name given to me by God, a name I longed to embody and continue to strive to live into. I bestow this name on you now, my son, not as some sort of demand for you to live up to, but a name to rest into. You already are Brave, and living into your name will be a reverent journey I look forward to being a part of.

I love you, son. I can't wait to meet you!

-Your Daddy

ACT ONE

GOOD FRIDAY

As a cloud vanishes and is gone, so is he who goes down to the grave and does not return, He will never come to his house again; his place will know him no more.

Job 7:9-10

We are Easter people living in a Good Friday world.

-Barbara Johnson

It's just another routine checkup. We laugh with our doctor, joking about Christy's newest way to "speed waddle." We all feel immense joy as we anticipate meeting our son, our Brave, now a week overdue.

As the doctor starts to listen for his heartbeat, the smile on her face is replaced by concern. She moves her stethoscope over Christy's belly. Slowly at first, then faster, frantically.

"Let me get another doctor to check you. I can't seem to find his heartbeat." The blood has drained from her face, though she is trying to remain professional.

My heart sinks into hell. "No, No, No," I say over and over, shaking my head as Christy and I stare at each other, horrified.

The new doctor enters the room in silence, listens, palpates Christy's belly. With a fragile hope in my eyes and a freight train of dread in my ears, I hear her say that our boy is curled up and we must get an ultrasound immediately to see if we can see his heart pump, to physically see if it is still beating or just hiding from us.

The room is silent. A collective holding of breath, no one heroic enough to exhale. The doctor pushes and presses on Christy's belly until an image appears. A motionless silhouette of our beautiful boy.

"I am sorry," she says.

We stare at the screen where our son's flawless silhouette lies, lifeless, in his mother's womb.

There is nowhere else to look. Where is a person supposed to look, I wonder, when death stares back?

- Andrew

They want me to go into labor, to give birth.

Not to life, but to death. They expect me to deliver my child's dead body into a world he will never know.

This is too much. How dare they ask me to do this? I can't. I must... push away his tiny hands and feet, pressing against my insides. This is the only way I will get to see him. This is the path I must take to hold my son.

I will take it. Despite my fear, I will run toward it, for my sake, for his sake, for our family's sake.

They give us a few instructions, telling us we have seventy-two hours before we need to come back to the hospital to deliver. They ask us if we have support, tell us that they can send a counselor if we need one.

Somehow I get myself dressed. Andrew and I cling to each other in utter disbelief. As we limp our way to the hallway and into the elevator, we are strangers to this world. Broken. Lost. Marked.

- Christy

We call a dear friend, screaming, "Brave is dead! We don't know what to do, we need you!" He yells back into the phone, "No! No! No! I am so sorry. We are coming. We will meet you at Andy and Lisa's house."

We hobble to our car with glazed eyes, trying to make sense of the senseless. Our words are few; we communicate with our moans.

After riding in shock for twenty minutes, we arrive at Andy and Lisa's house. I tumble out of the car into our friend Kevin's arms, wailing. Fifteen people awaiting our arrival turn into thirty, all howling and bawling for the next eight hours. Collective rage, fear, and shrieks of devastation make us feel as safe as we possibly can. Our friends give us room to express everything we feel.

There is no judgment.

We begin the wake before the wake as we wait to return to the hospital.

-Andrew

Accompanied by dear friends, we stumble back through the same hospital doors, we exited only two days before.

It's time. It's time to see glory and death displayed on one face. It's time to feel immense gratitude and fury, love and hate, grief and joy all at once. Gratitude that I get to see my boy for the first time, fury that he will not be alive when I do. Love like I have never felt, when I see his beauty, his perfection. I will also feel hate—that this is his story, that this is our story. I hate that the doctor went on vacation last week and we had to skip our originally scheduled appointment; maybe she would have seen something on the ultrasound, maybe she could have saved him, *maybe I could have saved him.* The "maybes" are already driving me insane.

The cold delivery room is as still as death, while we listen to people in other rooms crying out with life, glorious life. I pray that, miraculously, the doctors are wrong, that our brave little boy will defy all odds and enter this world wailing.

My dear friends Lisa and Alyssa prepare my body to be broken open. They massage my back as I try to breath deeply. They will remain with me throughout this entire process, his birth, his death, my death. Andrew is near, shattered to pieces. If only I could make his heart whole. We wait, we pray, we curse, we cry, we wait some more.

-Christy

One centimeter. It begins.

Two centimeters.
The Pitocin is beginning to work.

Three centimeters.
Contractions.
Progressing quickly, they say.
But time does not matter now.
We cannot save him.
Our baby is already gone.

Four centimeters.
I wonder what he will look like.

Five centimeters.
If I hurry, will it save him?

My water breaks. Down the sides of my legs it flows. I
whimper and shake.

Six centimeters.

There is nothing to hope for, nothing to breathe through. He has no breath.

Seven centimeters.

Not even the physical pain matters now.

The real pain is his lifeless body ... his lifeless future ... this deathly trick God has played on us.

Eight centimeters.

Harder contractions.

Drug me; I have felt enough. Make me numb. A long needle into my spine and I drift away, only vaguely aware of how my body convulses.

Nine centimeters.

I sleep, Andrew sleeping nearby, my dear friend Lisa holding me. Hours later I awake, hoping the nightmare has ended.

Ten centimeters.

They tell me it won't be long now.

The lights are low and my legs are raised and bent. Andrew kisses my forehead and commends my bravery. His face is less than an inch from mine, yet his words sound far away.

I hear another voice, God's voice perhaps, a voice of reassurance: "You can do this, Christy. You can do this."

I weep as I push—push my son's tiny body away from where he has spent almost ten months listening to our joyful anticipation.

Is this what is asked of the Eucharist?
For my body to be broken and poured out,
only to birth death?

This is Her body, broken for you.

-Christy

We spend the next twelve hours with our boy, gazing

into his flawless face, scavenging to memorize any curve
or detail we might have missed on his precious body.

Friends and relatives come, rushing to meet him for the
first and last time on this earth. We allow them to hold
him, bless him, cherish what was to be our beautiful gift
to the world.

My arms are greedy as our pastor takes him from me
to baptize his soul, still so alive I can feel it. An
awkward service begins. One by one, twenty or so
trembling hands touch Andrew and me, mourning
lips kiss Brave's face.

Our friend Andy reads a prayer. The words mean
something, I'm not sure what, but they mean
something they've never meant before.

As the water drips off Brave's tiny head,
the old life is gone.

The new life begins, away from us.
I did not want to baptize him this way.

To christen him into glory so reluctantly.

-Christy

The clock clicks to midnight; the time we'd agreed to give him back. But how? We just got him. We can't possibly return him. He is so perfect, so big, so beautiful.

My arms memorize the heft of his six pounds, thirteen ounces. I smell his soft skin, kiss his forehead, and touch his face. Oh, his sweet little face, so peaceful looking to have gone through such a war.

I don't have to look hard to see my own face in his lifeless form.

This is MY face; this is MY son.
The grief rips through me. I keep saying I'm sorry.

Sorry I did not save him.

Christy and I walk to the door, away from the friends

who witnessed his baptism. We stand behind a curtain and whisper words of love, tell him how much we love him, how horrific it is to give him away, trying our best to parent him, to let him know why he cannot stay with us.

With our wails as our prayers, my weak arms hold him out, away. Christy must help me. I tell him he is going to be safe, that the nurse loves him too. She kindly takes him and holds him close to her chest. As he leaves our sight I fall to floor in exhaustion and horror. *What have I done?! What good father would give away his son?*

Good Friday is an invitation to a holy and bloody lament.

With only unanswered questions on our tongues, can we remain in the grief until it is through with us?

I see nothing holy in this.

-Andrew

My body is wrecked from the labor, the delivery, the stitches, the loss of blood... but it is checking out of the hospital and walking to the car without our son in our arms that makes me break. We are not taking our child home where he belongs; we are not beginning this new chapter of life; his story of redemption we had longed for.

Only now do I notice the bloodstains on my legs and my clothes. I collapse onto the asphalt. Andrew holds me and we stay on the cold ground for what feels like forever, until I can make it to the car.

We cannot make ourselves go home. Instead, we drive straight from the hospital to the mortuary. We are led into a room and given funeral options and costs. We are asked to choose a coffin, a plot, and a date to bury him. I sign papers in a daze. Next we are led to a grassy hill in the cemetery called Babyland, truly the saddest place on earth.

This is where our son will be buried. We pick out his plot, next to another child named Scout. We hope they will be fast friends. I feel like I am looking at the backdrop for a horror film. This nightmare features us now. I cannot bear the injustice.

-Christy

My friend places the black veil on my head, carefully framing my salty, swollen face. They all help dress me in black. As I look around at these beloved friends, also wearing black, I remark that two years ago we were all standing together, each wearing white, as they dressed me for my wedding.

How can we be standing here again as they dress me for my firstborn's funeral? From a veil of white, the most beautiful day of my life, to a veil of black, the most tragic day.

God, what have You done?

-Christy

Christy and I reverently hold the handles of the little white casket and take the slowest steps of our lives. We can barely walk as we enter the silent sanctuary. Two hundred fifty people are waiting to meet our son. How can a room filled with so many people be so silent?

As we move forward, our wails echo throughout the old church. Our pastor and friends take turns speaking. Christy and I take turns sobbing as we lie prone below the altar, hands outstretched toward our child's coffin.

When the time comes for Christy and me to address the crowd, I do not know how we can possibly do it. Somehow I find words to thank our beautiful community for being with us. "Do not forget our precious boy," I plead. "May he inspire you live fully."

Sobbing, that is all I can muster. Christy echoes valiant words of thanks and heartache.

The street is blocked off as we walk Brave's body to the hearse. When we arrive at his sacred site, twenty of our closest friends and relatives are waiting in a line, like a small army ready to carry all three of us, should our legs fail.

Christy and I carry Brave's casket up the hill toward the hole carved into the ground. I stumble, nearly dropping him.

Our pastor says a few words. It's nearly impossible for me to stay in my body. I stare at the hole as our loved ones begin placing two hundred purple orchids from the funeral service into the earth, a receiving blanket for our baby. I pick up the coffin and lower my son into his sepulture. This small box holds so many dreams his mother and I had—for a son, a friend, a daughter-in-law, grandchildren, great-grandchildren. I am forced to bury them all with him, our most magnificent creation.

All I want to do is rip open his casket and kiss him and

touch him and hold his cold body close to mine.

Instead, I bury him with my hands.

The workers have dropped a pile of dirt a foot from the hole. I stop them from pushing it into the grave. I am his father. It is right that I do this for him.

I take dirt in my hands, then slowly open them and let it fall into the hole with my son inside. Christy joins me. One by one, friends and family begin to help us. The dirt hitting his casket makes a sound that I know will haunt me forever.

Our friend Heather holds out her hands, filled with dirt, near Christy's mouth. "Spit into my hands," she says. With tears and mucus running down her face, Christy spits into the dirt. Heather mixes the dirt with my wife's saliva, and then in the soil from the deepest grief we have known, she traces the sign of a cross in the mud. *Ashes to ashes, dust to dust.*

My hands, my suit, my face, my soul are dirty, and this feels as it should be. I dig harder into the soil, my hands caked with dirt and numb from the cold. I think of all the times I will not play in the dirt with Brave as he grows up. If this is the only time I will be able to spend time with my son in the dirt, I will cover myself in it.

We continue to bury our baby for the next forty-five minutes, eventually laying sod over the soil and standing by as a tractor smashes the grass flat. Each time the hammer-like tool hits the sod, it feels like my son is getting smashed. I feel my heart lurch in agony with each blow.

After about twenty blows, the ground is flat, and it looks as if nothing has happened here, as if our son never even existed.

Christy and I kiss the ground, rub it with our hands, hoping our child will rub off on us. No one else moves,

no one leaves the scene. Longing for a resurrection, I wait to see if the ground will rumble. Nothing. Our son is gone.

Our friends lay flowers, a teddy bear, and other

meaningful items on the grave. Slowly people begin making their way back to their cars. Christy and I limp down the dark hill, backwards, looking toward both the grave and the sky, wondering if Brave is watching, if he felt honored by us all, loved and delighted in.

I wonder if he is cold.

-Andrew

ACT TWO

HOLY SATURDAY

Something is over. In the deepest levels of my
existence something is finished, done.
My life is divided into before and after.

-Nicholas Wolterstorff, *A Lament for a Son*

No one ever told me that grief felt so like fear.

-C.S. Lewis, *A Grief Observed*

We awaken to the first morning of our life without

Brave. The winter begins, a dark world surrounds us. This is what life is to mean for us? To live with half of a heart? To forever face a gaping void in our family? I don't want to live in this new world. I want to die. It seems like the only way to be close my son.

But I cannot escape this agony; I cannot run, despite how much I want to. There is no place to go. "Go to God," so many have said. How do I go to the one by whom I feel most betrayed? The one to whom I have dedicated my work and my life? The God who set us up for the tease of a lifetime--who *is* this God?

I get out the pictures we took of Brave at the hospital yesterday. I can't tear my eyes away from his beauty, his perfection.

How cruel to show us something so exquisite and

then take him away. I don't know how I can bear this brave new world without him.

-Andrew

Our community is made up of incredible souls. Andy and Lisa have opened up their entire house, and people are constantly coming over, staying for a few minutes or for hours, depending on their commitments and their comfort level with grief. Our friends and relatives have flown in from all over the world to be with us. They are lying near us, crying with us, silent with us—and in very small moments which feel a bit irreverent, they are smiling with us.

Andrew and I wander from the living room to the bedroom like zombies, unsure of what to do. When we are overwhelmed by our grief, we cry until there are no more tears, for the moment. People are kind, touching us, rubbing our backs and our hands and our hair. It is as if our own bodies are corpses and our friends are the pallbearers, carrying us through our anguish. We know little of what this type of mourning takes. So we just wander around, still in shock, wondering what to do next. Our loved ones do the same.

We are asked countless times if we need anything. We always give the same answer: nothing. This is what is true of grief: you truly want nothing in the world except what has been lost.

My family brings us all of our favorite foods, beers, candies. Nothing soothes our constant sickness. Any tinge of delight feels like a betrayal of our son.

But on this fifth night of mourning, the fire has gone out and Andrew actually asks for something. Would someone mind getting more firewood? "And," he adds quietly, "maybe some of those chocolate chip ice cream sandwiches?"

My heart takes its first shallow breath and I smile. My precious, courageous husband is still alive, and that means something else: I am still alive. Barely, but alive Chris brings back four stacks of firewood and three large boxes of ice cream sandwiches.

We each take one, maybe only to remind ourselves that we are all still here.

-Christy

We have to design Brave's headstone.

What do you do when every moment demands a task that should never have to be done? You design a headstone.

We call it Brave's marker; that is easier to say than headstone. We are always looking for easier words.

"He is gone."
"We lost him."
"He died" is much too raw.

So, marker it is, instead of headstone.

We start by drawing trees.
Our name, Bauman, means tree.

So we draw three trees, Brave's tree in the middle, of course—a baby tree nestled between two larger ones, Andrew and me.

Then we decide that birds will fly from Brave's tree.
Three days before he died, I finished a piece art for
his nursery of birds flying across the sky.

I will get them tattooed on my abdomen,
near my womb, flying away.

Now, what words do we have engraved?
How many words can you fit on 13x18 stone?
How do you squeeze in, "BRAVE! Come back, love,
please don't go, we love you, a million times we love
you, and a day will not go by that we won't realize we
were not meant to live on this earth without you!"

There is not enough room,
not enough time,
not enough space in our hearts for one more drop of
sorrow.

So, we decide on this:

"Even eternity will not give us enough time. We miss
you and love you deeply. –Mom and Dad."

-Christy

I have so much father in me. I do not know what to do with its excess. How do I wear this new skin of fatherhood when I cannot hold my son?

I will not teach him how to walk, mow the yard, throw a ball, shoot a basket, write a poem, talk to a woman, be kind, or love others well. I won't see him take his first steps or graduate college. I have a lifetime of nevers ahead, a lifetime of should-have-beens.

No man should be asked to live this story. To have so much father in him and not know where to put it.

- Andrew

Jesus...oh Jesus...help me, I can't do this...

It has been nearly two weeks since we lost our son. This is my first prayer since God said "no" to raising Brave from the dead.

Father, why have you forsaken me?
Yet where else can I go but to you? You have the words of life.

Come Lord Jesus, please come...please return to us quickly.
This is not our home.

Come back and wipe every tear from our eyes.
Place our baby in my arms again and reign here on this earth.

Your will be done, on Earth as it is in heaven.

-Christy

Hooray, he is here, God is good!

A friend's social media post announces the arrival of their newborn son. I am still frozen in time, in the room where my son was born, lifeless. Not to a grand "Hooray, God is good," but to torment like nothing I have ever known. How dare she?

Of course, her delight is good, and her status update was not directed at me, but my innocence has been lost. My son is not here, and God may not be so good after all.

Right after Brave was born, I received an email from old friend who told me that during his morning quiet time with God he heard that we would have another son, and then he added some obscure Bible verse at the end of the email. Does this person have any idea what he said?

I don't want another son! I want the son I lost! My friend's well-intentioned words pour salt into my bloody lacerations.

If you have the courage to walk with us through this unspeakable evil, please don't give me answers. I don't want your pat Bible verses or your lofty promises of prayer. No, I want something much darker than that. I ask you to suffer, to take the nails of my grief and drive them into yourself. I ask you to shut your mouth, and open your hands. Don't say you understand. Wail as I wail; curse as I curse; pray as I pray. Kneel with me by my bed feeling useless and helpless… Yes, for then you will understand a part of me that few have the courage to know.

I realize that this will cost you greatly, but deep down, I will learn my worth from the measure of your sacrifice.

-Andrew

She started handing me leaves of cabbage the day

after I came home from the hospital. Green cabbage,

purple cabbage, to put across my chest, to help my

milk dry up.

Milk that had built up in my breasts to feed my baby.

My baby is not here.

For three weeks I have have been wearing a tight
fitting bra, replacing cabbage.

Every four hours, new cabbage.

To take away the food I have made for him.

But milk still comes, rebelling, demanding to feed my

baby.

Let's put in more cabbage.
You need more cabbage.

Cabbage.

Cold cabbage.

Wilting cabbage.

Damn this infernal purple cabbage.

I stare into the bathroom mirror,

cursing my naked reflection.

Stop! Stop trying to feed him!

There is a knock on the door.

I open it.

There is more cabbage in her hands.

- Christy

It makes no difference to me how many days' have

gone by. Every day is just another day I have to bear the

brutal truth: We have lost our firstborn son.

I had to look at him dead.

I had to hold him, cold and ashen.

I had to lay him in the ground.

His car seat sits empty.

His room is still and void.

His crib is waiting, confused.

His clothes are folded neatly and untouched.

My arms are empty.

God raised his son after three days.

Even God could not bear to look at his son dead.

God only had to wait three days.

I will wait a lifetime.

My life is no longer my life,

my thoughts are no longer my
thoughts, my heart is no longer my
heart. They all belong to my son,
whose body now resides in the ground.
My heart, my soul, my life, buried with him.

-Andrew

Come back, son! I sob into my pillow. "Please

come back!" Maybe if God doesn't give us more than we can handle, he will see me now and give him back to us. I repeatedly dream that I will be at the grave and hear him crying in the ground, and I will dig him up and he will be alive in my arms. I still believe at times that God can bring him back. But each day his body grows colder and my lips are heavier with withheld kisses.

I don't know how to contain this much longing. It will only grow as time passes, and eventually my heart will stop.

Or worse, my heart will not stop. It will keep beating, forcing me to live every day with yearning for my precious little boy.

I just want to break things. There are not enough broken things in this world. A world that desperately avoids its brokenness is no world at all for me. A gospel that avoids death is not good news. To live honestly is to live in the messy truth that joy and sorrow inhabit the same heart.

Heartbreak and torture dance with laughter and joy. This is the paradox that few have the courage to hold.

Do I?

-Christy

There are four infants on this flight home for

Christmas. They mock me with their loud cries and
sweet haunting laughter. This is hell. Every day is hell
without my son in my arms. I would not wish this
torture on my worst enemies.

Christmas will never be a season of joy again. The
multiple times I've heard "Merry Christmas!" already
today make me want to scream. *Don't you know I buried
my child sixteen days ago with my bare hands? Can't you see that
this Christmas is anything but merry?!* This is a grave
Christmas, in every sense of the word.

I know now why people go crazy in the aftermath of
tragedy. I feel crazy. The world is going on around me
and I am not. I died with Brave.

So, do not tell me "Merry Christmas." Do not remind

me of sugar plums and childlike wonder and festively wrapped gifts waiting under the tree. The newborns surrounding me already torture me enough with thoughts of my baby son, whose eyes are closed forever under the cold, dark ground.

-Andrew

This day was going to be the highlight of the year.

Waking up with him to the magic and wonder of Christmas morning, our greatest gift in our arms. This was to be his first Christmas, our first as a family. Could a day when the world celebrates birth be any crueler? We are living crucifixion, not birth. Jesus' birth held so much hope, deliverance, and promise of life to come. Our Christmas is a day of death, hope destroyed, tears, and longing to hold our boy.

Is it okay that we would rather die right now than continue on like this? I know our family is worried about us; I'm sure they are discussing our mental health. As kind as they have been, at times I feel judgment mixed with desire for us to "move on." Sadly, I know this is only the beginning. They don't understand that we must grieve at the depths to which we loved him. If we are to be even semi-normal and functional ever again, our grief must be entered fully. It must be raw and loud. Our love for our son demands it.

This Christmas is not one of hope or celebration, so Christy and I hibernate in our bedroom at her parent's house. We hold each other, sharing what could have been, how close we almost were.

-Andrew

After an agonizing Christmas, we fly to North

Carolina. The mountains are my safe place. They may even be big enough to hold my grief. We inhale the forest, breathing the fresh air and attempting to suture together the pieces of our broken bodies.

All I can think of is you, my son—how I long to see your delight as you experience all things new, how I never got to see your smile or the hear sound of your giggle. There is so much I wanted to show you here, where I grew up. I looked forward to taking you to the cold streams where we could stomp together, go camping at my favorite spot, watch your joy in seeing your first waterfall, hike the ridges and share with you the peace I have found in these woods.

I mourn those stories never to be told, those dreams

never to come true. There is a hollowness inside my bones that I have no idea what to do with. I keep trying to feel it so I can try to honor it, but it is impossible to bear for long.

We were not made to look at death. We were made to bask in life.

That is why beauty captivates us so, shimmering in front of us.

You should be here sharing this beauty with me.

I miss you so much, my son.

-Andrew

Last night we ventured to Wal-Mart at midnight to

avoid the crowds and cash in a gift card Christy's mom
gave us for Christmas. After an hour and a half of
wandering back and forth and almost leaving four
times, we ended up with a box of Reese's Puffs cereal
and cappuccino mix. Every time we buy something we
feel as though we're trying to buy off our son; trying to
stop the pain through material consumption.

It doesn't work.

Later we lay wide awake in bed, utterly exhausted by our
mourning. Most nights since we lost Brave we fall
asleep with the TV on, anything to quiet the relentless
voices in our heads.

"You could have done something; you could have saved
him. You should have known he was in trouble. A good

father…mother…would have … should have…" Fill in the blank. My voices of self-contempt are loud and at times debilitating.

On nights when we are courageous enough to try to fall asleep naturally, our sorrow erupts into weeping. The silence of the night reminds us so vividly of our loss. Our words turn cold toward each other, and the smallest hint of dissention only makes us that more desperate. If one of us leaves the room, the other quickly follows in the dark; we don't want to be left alone, at least no more alone than we already feel since he died.

So, in the wee hours of this new year—so cruel with taunts of hope amidst fresh death—I make a fire and we weep in each other's arms on the living room floor until we fall into restless sleep. We wake around noon to find that snow has fallen, but our usual delight is absent. We each have the same thought: *The grave. Snow on the grave. Our baby's body…so cold.*

"It's Brave's first snow," I say, as we drive to the

cemetery.

The hillside is blanketed in white. Reverently, we walk over and begin clearing Brave's grave.

We light new candles and replace the old.

We talk to him about snow and find ourselves looking up at the sky more than at the ground. It is a maddening game we play now, uncertain of how to honor the physical body we made, now lying in the cold earth. There is no solace in the thought that his spirit is elsewhere, welcomed and warm.

Our silence at the graveside is awkward. We have no words to say to each other. So we speak our love to him and then quietly walk back to the car, heartsick that our son's first snow lies on top of him.

-Andrew

His hair is falling into the bathroom sink.

The buzzing drowns out my whimpering as tears streak down my face. I will never see my little boy grow up to watch his father perform this ritual.

Shaving. I will never watch his daddy teach him how to be a man.

I have so much anger, such fierce rage welling up within me. I often yell, pull out my hair, break things, tear my clothes, trace my forehead with ashes as tears spill down my cheeks.

God has turned His face away from me. He hates me.

My pain has shifted from disbelief to wailing to depression. Everything I see, everything I look at, reminds me of something we could have shown, taught, or offered our son.

I feel robbed. I know there is no escaping this. We will always be without something, no matter what treasures we have in this life, no matter how many blessings.

We have been cheated.

Evil was creeping around our story,
waiting until all was sure to be well,
and then strangling my son in my womb.

I do not want to look at you, God, I only want to rage at you.

Where were your strong arms, mighty to save? You allowed destruction and death to swallow up our child.

You could have saved him. You knew what he meant to me. You are cruel.

What else can you steal from me?

I am already dead.
I am not chosen.

I am not blessed.

I am not with child anymore.

You have given me a grave instead of a son.

-Christy

It is so hard to think of his sweet body in the ground.

Many times over the past six weeks I have had to convince my hands not to dig him back up, so I can hold him for just one more moment.

My damn hands, you are the hands that held him tightly for only those few precious hours. You are the traitorous hands that gave him away to the nurse at midnight.

You cursed hands, you are the hands that picked up the dirt over and over and over again. You are the hands that opened up wide to drop the earth on top of him.

You are the gentle hands that would have and did care for him so tenderly.

You are the reverent hands that held his brave little

broken body so honorably.

You are the brave hands that placed him in the ground and covered him so caringly.

You are the fortunate hands that got to hold him for a short time so lovingly.

I love my hands, for they touched glory.

-Andrew

I don't know which was more horrific—the moment we realized you were no longer breathing, or the moment we saw your face.

Oh, the awe of seeing my face in your face, seeing your daddy's face in your face. I studied your tiny fingers; they did not look like mine, they looked just like your father's. I studied your body, your broad shoulders to which we both contributed, your perfect torso, your sweet legs. Your toes…I had to check your toes to see if you had a webbed one like your dad; but no, your toes looked just like mine.

I don't know if I will ever have the courage to chance it all again, after such a torturous few hours with you. The risk seems too great. How could we ever again wait nine months with eager anticipation and wild hope?

Apparently, my heart will keep beating today, though I don't know how. We will have to move on, to dream differently. But we will always bear the scars of what those hours with you cost us.

-Christy

I should wear a sign telling others to beware, that somehow I am a magnet for suffering. My life is dark today, my faith even darker. My questions are as angry and confused as my answers.

Many of my friends seem not to have suffered much. Their parents are still together, they have multiple children, good jobs, and their lives, their questions, their gospel are uncomplicated. My parents are not together. I have been addicted. My son is buried beneath the earth. I am broken. I feel as if I wear a scarlet letter, *S*, for Sufferer.

I thought I had suffered enough in my life. I already knew pain; I already knew what it is like to lose. Oh, how I wish there were a suffering quota; a point at which once you have experienced a certain amount of pain, you are released from it.

-Andrew

Fifty-five days have passed.

One thousand, three hundred and twenty hours have slipped away.

It still aches to go to his grave, to go out in public, to see his empty room.

Everywhere I go, I am aware that Brave could be with me.

Strapped to my chest, sleeping in a crib or car seat. He could go anywhere with us.

But he never will.

I remember feeling like pregnancy would last forever.

In those last weeks, I thought my child would never come.

How I longed to see his face, hear his cry! Then Evil

decided that we would not meet him until eternity.

We would grow old longing to have known him.

We would, in fact, be pregnant forever.

So much sadness. So little we can do.

The days move madly on, hopelessness dogging our every step.

Depression like water pools at our front door.

We can't get around it, can't get over it, so we just close the door and sit on the couch.

I don't want to get over it. I am so scared I will never get over it.

Andrew is looking at a picture of us on a hike with friends, all of us laughing and vibrant. Andrew's eyes are bright and my grin is confident. It almost hurts to look at these faces, our faces of old.

"Were we just naïve then?" my husband asks. I don't know how to answer him. Death has left its mark on us.

Death has stolen from our family. I am quiet as I stare at the picture.

"Maybe we were just hopeful," I say, "and now we must be brave."

-Christy

I have not always been attuned to what it feels like to

be an outsider. I am a middle class, educated, privileged, white male who has normally fit into society without much effort.

But now I feel my outsider-ness acutely. Now Christy and I are marked by death; not only death, but the death of our child.

We are the couple that incites heartache. People speak softly, some not knowing what to say, so they do not say a word.

Others allow their discomfort to cause them to say careless, strange things.

Many speak to soothe their own anxiety, not ours.

Our closest friends are having a get-together today. We have changed our minds about going eight times in the past fifteen minutes.

"Kids are going to be there, I just wanted to let you know," our friend had said kindly.

I was reminded again of our differentness. I would rather he tell us, show concern, yet it stings all the same. There are few things more isolating than grief. To posture oneself in the world in such a way that honors both death and life, joy and sorrow, comes at a cost.

I am coming to see that part of the cost is becoming a foreigner—never feeling quite home, always feeling strangely unwelcome in one's own skin.

-Andrew

The damp frost seeps through the seat of my jeans as I sit on the black smiling lip of the swing. I curl my fingers around the slippery chains and begin to sway, back and forth, back and forth. Because it is after midnight, Andrew is waiting in the car at the edge of the park to make sure I am safe.

I haven't stopped crying for the past three hours, and I don't know where else to go but to this place where I carried Brave so many times, alive in my womb.

I can't stay home; I can't keep being reminded of his absence. I can't write any more tortuous words of pain.

I feel the wind creep under my coat and run down my tear soaked chest. I am so angry, so full of rage. *Don't you know I can't hold this?! It is too much! Too much!*

ANDREW & CHRISTY BAUMAN

I swing harder, much harder, for my dialogue with God has just begun. The wind whips my hair, stinging my face as I sob.

You have given me death for a son. While all the other sons live, you let mine rot. You let his little body decompose back into the dirt that I buried him in with my own hands. I trusted you! But you have stolen my hope and allowed me to be mocked. You have dashed my hope in your goodness, your faithfulness, your love. You have left me with dust.

I don't know what to do but swing.

Finally, I stop and start to walk back to the car. Whirling around, I grab the swing and throw it again and again as hard as I can against the poles, letting the crashing sound echo through the silent neighborhood. I do not want to stop, but after long enough, I do finally stop; I stop because I realize that nothing will bring him back and nothing will dull my pain.

It will be a long lifetime, a very long lifetime to hope and long for Glory.

-Christy

There is a rhythm to grief.

A rhythm that keeps us from losing our minds.
Our cadence of survival is starting to take shape.

We take a walk in the woods.
We go to Brave's grave.
We journal and weep.

Sometimes, if tears come again, we write more.
Then, we are exhausted.

There are no more words to be written, no more tears
to be shed, no more asking God why.

Comfort is what we need in these moments. We are
so tender, still moving around without skin on.

The world's joy is too loud. So, we still wince a little
when we venture outside of the house.

We feel depleted after someone comes to visit. Mourning requires more than I ever imagined, more than I ever wanted to know.

Mourning requires a kindness to my fragility. The world tells me to move on, but my grief tells me to move in, lean in deeper, and make grief my friend. The paradox that few understand is that the only way out of grief is through it. I must listen to my body as it guides me in this time of heartache.

-Andrew

Tonight I lie in the darkness and think about what it would be like if my baby were still here. I wish my nights were interrupted with his cries so I could soothe or feed him. I picture his sweet little face and his perfect form. The tears begin to pool beneath my eyelashes. I start praying, asking God to take care of him. I ask him to comfort me now, since my little one is probably okay.

The tears flow harder as I slip out of bed to the bathroom so I don't wake up my husband. I sit on the cold edge of the tub with my feet propped up against the toilet. The apologies begin to flood out of my mouth.

"I'm sorry, God, for whatever I did wrong. I'm so sorry that my body didn't know my baby was in trouble." The apologies and the tears come faster and faster.

I grab a cold rag and wipe my face, trying to mother myself because there is no baby to be mothered.

I need a mother.

I need someone to tell me how they lost their child, had life stripped from their womb and survived.

I think of Mary. I think of how she had to watch her son be beaten and nailed to a tree.

I didn't have to watch my son suffer.

God have mercy on the parent who must watch her child suffer. Mary did and, somehow, survived.

I critique my body in the mirror. What price will it have to pay before I can care for it again?

Oh womb, how long?

I can hear my uterus wailing as it retracts, wondering what it did wrong.

But then a current of compassion ripples through.

"You did nothing wrong, my love. You did nothing

wrong. You cared for Brave so well, you held him so gloriously. I will bless you, my body, as I curse the unknown that took our baby from us. You are free from my judgment and condemnation. You are free to mourn with me."

-Christy

Normally my anger is subversive and subtle.

Now it is always at the surface, easily accessible.
I frequently imagine swinging my wooden baseball bat at fragile things.

Last night I yelled at Christy. I knew my anger was misplaced, but I chose to lash out anyway. She cried, then I broke down. I knew I was wrong and apologized and wept for hours as I felt my heart re-breaking.
We fell asleep on the living room floor, myself face first in my own drool and tears.

Many marriages fail in light of such stinging loss. How will Christy and I survive? Will we survive?

I believe so. No other person knows my heartache and longing the way my wife does. Where else can we go but to each other? We will press on, not one day at a time, for that sounds terribly exhausting, but literally one second at a time as we try to limp our way toward a new equilibrium. My hope is that we can fumble our way into a life where we can love each other easily again, dream unabashedly, dance to new rhythms with a pleasure we barely remember.

-Andrew

I watch her, our two-year-old marriage, as she tries to make sense of what is going on. She rages when we try to explain to her that Brave died. She beats her fists against our chests. It is heart-wrenching to watch her anguish. She feels marred, as if in her boldest and most vulnerable attempt to create something beautiful, she failed utterly.

This is why I cannot allow my body to feel pleasure at my husband's nearness, why I can't offer my broken beauty for a moment of love.

Sex is what brought us to this place of bloodshed; why would I make a move toward the act that led us to the hope of Brave, only to leave us alone with each other?

To entertain even the thought of my own pleasure is impossible. Every time I look at my husband, I see my son's face.

But the truth is, my body was magnificent in growing and birthing a baby. The love between my husband and me is most beautiful when we are dreaming and creating. To deaden myself to his touch is to despise the best thing about us.

So, as I stand in front of the mirror preparing to take a bath, I stare at my reflection.

My bloated and stretch-marked abdomen. My breasts, once engorged and yearning. With tears rolling down my cheeks, I tell them they did a magnificent job, and they must heal.

When Andrew comes to bed, I see the huge gash down his chest as he removes his pierced armor. I see the blood oozing from his head and lips, but he still stands there, miraculously alive. He is holding Marriage; she is crying on his shoulder, and his blood is running down her arm.

Andrew reaches for my hand and I come near. Marriage kisses my face and whispers in my ear, "I am the love that created the most beautiful thing you have ever known." My sweet little boy, his body so perfect, so beyond what I could have imagined it would look like.

He took my breath away.

Marriage, thank you. I will kiss the mirrored image of my late son's face. I will bless my husband.

In the midst of this bloodshed and grief, I will bless myself.

-Christy

How do I bless the beauty we created?

If I live shallowly from this moment on, will that honor my boy? No.

But I want to cower, I want to hide. To open my heart could mean being vulnerable again to great torment. How could I ever lose one more person I care about? Even my sweet lab I pet differently now than before.

With each stroke of his yellow coat I am telling him to never leave me, that I need him to be okay. How can I bear even one more tear?

How can I have one more day of visiting my son's tomb, which is now his cradle?

I have nearly forgotten how to desire since Brave fell asleep forever. The world is gray and I am dim. Where did my once-passionate, desirous heart go? I fear it leaped into the coffin with my child. My desire for him was otherworldly. I had so many plans for him, for my family. So much hope—oh yes, so much desire. But now the light and weight of desire is wrapped in the broken body of my precious boy. He holds my desire in his tiny hands.

How will I ever resurrect it? Is it as impossible as resurrecting my son? I do not know.

I do know that one day, to bless the beauty we created, I must live fully again. Differently, but fully.

I must be brave enough to allow my desire to become ravenous again. To blaze with hope for resurrection.

I must.

-Andrew

Before my son died, I didn't really need God to be

Mother-God.

The words sounded awkward on my tongue,
and the dismissal I would have received from my
denomination did not make it worth pondering.

Although I like the idea of God being a mother,
I did not need God to be Mother. Until I lost
my baby.

When your child is taken from you,
when your arms are empty after ten months of your
womb being full, you need God to be a Mother.

When you feel your baby's milk dry up in your
breasts, you not only need God to be Mother, you
demand God to be Mother.

You require it so as not to lose your faith.

-Christy

Our grief ebbs and flows. There are moments when I can actually laugh, make a silly comment, or hear Andrew's chuckle, and I feel like we might be okay, in time.

And just as quickly I am struck by some small sound, comment, or even smell that sucker punches me in the gut. The tears come suddenly and I am reminded that I am walking around without skin on. These are the moments when silence is heart-wrenching, laughter is excruciating, and words are enraging.

Life feels so very fragile, so very delicate, so very stolen. I want to be single again, just married again. I want to not be able to feel Brave's small kicks against my abdomen.

I want to be content and without hate.

I don't want to wear the lines of death upon my face. I want time to run past us; age us quickly so the severity of our son's death is not so raw.

But this morning I was reminded of why I love the man I married.

"We must make peace with ourselves," he said, "and peace with God."

When these words tumbled out of his mouth, the smallest hope settled into my heart that we might survive this.

I don't know where peace will come from, yet if there is a space where my hatred for death and for all it stole from Brave and my family can co-exist with life and breath; if my unresolved heartache, my unrequited love, can learn to dance to a bearable rhythm for the next sixty years of my life... maybe peace will come.

-Christy

I visit Brave's grave alone today.

Beautiful trinkets placed by friends cover the holiest of ground I know on this earth. My warm, salty tears mix into the cold, wet ground.

I still can't comprehend that his death is a reality. My anger toward God has been so fierce. For the first time, today, I wonder if my anger makes Brave confused. If God is the one taking care of him now, then does my anger toward God make Brave question whether or not he is in good hands?

"God is good, Brave...you can trust him," I whisper. I press my lips to the ground, saying it over and over. I'm not sure if I am saying it loud enough to be heard through the packed dirt, so I yell it this time. "God is good, Brave! I know that I'm angry with him right now because I miss you so much, but you can trust him!" I burrow my face into the place where I think his small casket lies. I am crying so hard that I no longer feel the cold wind around me or the grass in my mouth or the wet ground seeping into my clothes.

"God is good! God is good! You can trust him!"
I yell it over and over until I am sure he has heard.

-Andrew

Three months have gone by, but still, if I am left alone with my thoughts for too long, I go crazy.

Anger.
Blame.
Guilt.

I want to know if God knew this was going to happen. I want to know why Evil is so cruel. I want to know why we fight so hard, if Good does not win.

Does it come down to this? Good and Evil? Or is it fate? Karma?

I used to believe that good things happen to good people. So, did I do something wrong?

Did I somehow bring this upon us?

Did I not pray enough?

Should I have done something, anything, in the hours before he died?

I wonder if he suffered.

Did he just go to sleep when the cord wrapped tight around his neck? Or did he kick in panic? I cannot bear the thought of that horror.

The unanswerable questions taunt me, haunt me. I can't breathe in these moments. I forget that I am still alive. I have to coach myself to take a breath. To live for more than my son. I must live for myself. I must live for my husband. I must live for the family and friends around me who make this world such a beautiful place. I must train myself to breathe through the pain, to massage it and lean into it.

Perhaps my labor to bring Brave into this world can teach me something about surviving a future without him. As each contraction came during the delivery, my body would automatically tense up with pain, my muscles would involuntarily constrict and I would have to consciously massage them until they relaxed. I had others around me continually, helping me to coach myself to breathe through the pain and let it wash over me.

I'm reminded of how, when I first learned to surf, I fought the powerful current. But when I let the wave pull my body under and scrape me against the sand, it would eventually deliver me to shore. The same was true with my contractions; the pain would deliver me to the end of each wave, and then I could breathe deeply before the next came rushing in.

Caught in these waves of mourning, I am overwhelmed with heartache.

But when I let my body scream out in pain, allow the tears to stream down my face, and all the memories of Brave's lost life to flood through my mind, I let the wave take me.

I know there will be another breath for me.

-Christy

*This is especially for Andrew, that you might find comfort
wherever you can.*

These words are attached to a McDonald's gift card
inside one of seven bags of Trader Joe's groceries.

My husband's lips are moving as he reads these words,
and then I see him smile. Warmth floods my heart. His
smile reminds me that we are still alive and we are still
breathing and we still have love. It makes me believe, if
only for a moment, that we might make it through this
nightmare.

Maybe it's not your fault, God.

Maybe you wail *with* us.

Maybe your omnipotence does not mean that you rush
in and save the day when Evil attacks and appears to
win. Maybe my anger needs to be directed at the Evil

One, not at you.

Yet, somehow it's easier to be pissed at you.

Because somewhere deep down I trust in your goodness.

I trust that you can handle my anger and hold my rage and still love me.

When an injustice takes place, we all want to hold someone or something accountable. I have wrestled with you and I will continue to, but will I have the same strength to wrestle with Evil?

I hope so. Perhaps Evil will not win in the end. Glory will.

-Christy

Be restored. This is what he says when he greets us.

We have just been seated at a table in his restaurant, Canlis, the nicest, most expensive restaurant in Seattle.

We figured out that we can afford to eat there occasionally if we order from the bar menu. Tonight is a rare night out to dinner since losing Brave. We have brought my sister with us to thank her for taking care of us daily through our darkest nights. "Be restored," our friend tells us, as if offering a sacrament.

Earlier I had dressed for the night in the same dress I had worn the last time we were there with Brave. We had come twice in the past year. Once, when we had just found out we were pregnant but had not told anyone yet, and again three nights before we lost Brave. At the graveside this evening, we told Brave we were going to Canlis, and I reminded him that he had been

there with us twice and how much he had enjoyed dancing to the live music. *Oh Lord, I miss my little one. What does it mean to be restored?*

I have no answer yet, but these two sacred words gently wash over me throughout the evening as many times as my hand reaches down to touch my empty womb. *Be restored.*

-Christy

Sometimes I want to say it out loud, in a conversation at the most random moments.

"I miss Brave."

I want to say it again and again in case people have forgotten him, so I don't dishonor him by withholding his name. I must remind others that he was here.

Their babies are growing every day, bringing more joy and fullness to their lives. Every day I am reminded that I cannot see Brave grow or change.

Every day I wonder where he is. I hope he is experiencing what I imagine, but, truthfully, it is a weak consolation. Prayer is still sporadic on my tongue. Sometimes when I pray I feel only angry and skeptical. *You who knit him together in my womb,*

where is your anger, your regret, your sorrow?
Where can I find you weeping?

But then I think, *Jesus must know my pain.* He has to understand the absolute helplessness and consuming grief I feel. What else could have caused him to endure death? What else could have kept him on the cross?

I picture him being beaten, mocked by Evil. What was he thinking of that gave him the resolve to stay, to let them rip his flesh apart? He must have had to constantly remind himself why he was there; continually bring to mind why he was allowing their hatred to nail those stakes into his limbs. He must have been thinking of the hundreds of Jews being tortured, of the widows and orphans…and us.

I am almost afraid to be so proud to think he thought of Brave, Andrew, and me…but I can't help but wonder, did our faces flash through his mind? Did we even for a moment give him courage to stare death in the face and let Evil take him with its hideous and malicious hands?

I realize that I am shouting inside on Jesus' behalf. "You can do this, Lord!" I am echoing the words he spoke to me on my darkest night, in the hospital room, as I brought Brave into this world.

"You can do this, Christy!"

It is finished.

-Christy

ACT THREE

RESURRECTION

I remember the man who said "no" to false power,
who died and rose again— And I know that his story
is also my story, the story of all of Creation: We die
that we may live.

-Mandy Hughes

But this I know for sure: as long as we're alive,
choosing resurrection is always worth the risk.

-Parker Palmer

Resurrection asks us to live out Christ's heroic triumph, trusting that Good will have the final say in the aftermath of death. But as Easter approaches this year, talk of resurrection is almost offensive to my broken heart. How do I celebrate a risen savior as I continue to mourn at the tomb of my buried son?

Part of me believes that Sunday will dawn in my weary soul.

But the truth is, I continue to rage.

Andrew rages.

What do we do with this anger? It feels so un-Christian, so unlike the old me.

The innocent me.

Andrew has music playing in the bathroom. I hear

familiar Christian songs blaring through the door. Songs that once made me fall to my knees in worship.

I open my mouth, attempting to form the lyrics of old. Words of praise and thanksgiving. But my mouth feels full of sawdust. I cannot say what they say.

After ten years of leading worship, the loss of my child has taken the song out of me. I long for the days when I sang with abandon. It was easier to worship before there was grief. But now, sorrow colors my praise and the words get caught in my throat.

I ask God if I can skip Easter this year. The Good Friday service was more in keeping with my reality.

God, please forgive me if I can't celebrate.

I will try my best to honor you and the death and resurrection of your Son.

I will honor it because it is my only hope, the reason I will see my own son again. I know it is the best part of the gospel story. I know it is the best part of Brave's story.

But I can't face going to church. I will honor the resurrection at the cemetery, next to my son's dead body. I don't want him to feel alone. Come Easter morning, Jesus, I will go to his tomb, like Mary did early that day, waiting, wondering, mourning, and hoping.

I will watch and wait.

Selah.

-Christy

Our healing does not look like I thought it would.

In fact, nearly eight months since burying our son, our healing does not even look much like healing. It looks more like survival.

Every day we get out of bed, tie our shoes, and bless that as enough. At times getting out of bed is the greatest act of faith and courage we can muster, but we declare it sufficient.

What does it mean to learn to live again? To rise after such a bloody crucifixion? To courageously follow in the painful steps of Jesus?

I don't want to just survive; I want to live fully. The pain will last a lifetime, but it is softening, just a bit. There are moments now when I catch myself laughing again. It always surprises me. A wave of guilt usually follows. I have to remind myself that my son wants me to experience joy; yes, he wants me to live, he needs me to live.

To live again does not mean to forget, it does not mean not to feel longing or pain—actually, quite the opposite. It means to fully surrender, to become deeply familiar with both pain and desire, not to be consumed by it, but to know it intimately. To see, hear, smell, taste, and touch my deepest fear and sorrow is to become a friend to my longing for my son. Yes, this is what I will strive to attain. This is what it means for me to live resurrected.

So, our healing will look like not giving up. Our healing will look like living within a larger story.

Our healing will mean learning to walk with a limp, forever changed, forever marked, forever stumbling toward resurrection, all the while allowing our son and the pain of his absence to matter.

-Andrew

There are rainbows of light spilling through the prism we hang in our living room window.

The rainbows have been beaming at me all week, beckoning me to notice them, to kiss them when they momentarily rest on my husband's face. I am desperate to see each one, as if Brave himself is sending them to me. The rainbows also beckon me to believe and hope, to tell the world that I miss and love my son, but I still live.

Anne Lamott says that "sometimes we need to tend to the inside through the outside."

This is what my friend wrote on the note clipped to a bag of pampering items she delivered to me this morning.

I still feel guilty pampering myself. I feel guilty when I put on makeup and try to feel beautiful. Shouldn't I keep looking like a mother who lost her child?

I want to snatch back laughter the second I hear it dance off my lips because it feels like a betrayal of my baby's short existence. My very survival feels like I've cheated death, while he didn't have a chance to do so.

And yet, in this season of full bloom, I am having more days when my living feels like it honors his precious life. My joy and laughter echo the larger truth that we live to love and be loved. Andrew and I are learning to turn toward each other without tears. We are finding comfort in our shared grief, so deeply understood by the other. A new kind of mourning has emerged, an honoring of the parts of us we buried with Brave. We realize that new growth and new life have emerged from the ash heap, and on our best days we remind each other that we have a braver and wilder love than we ever had before.

So, I will try to pamper myself today as a small expression of my faith in goodness.

May my beauty reflect my son's perfect face.

-Christy

Equinox occurs when daylight and darkness are equal, when the center of the sun can be observed directly overhead, and the tilt of Earth's axis is inclined neither away from nor toward the sun. A day of rest, a day of not moving ahead or behind, as if God decided that Earth itself needed a day to rest up before changing direction.

Our last autumn equinox turned us naively toward winter, not only tilting us toward shorter and colder days, but to the darkest night of our souls.

Our feet have grown weary traveling back and forth to our son's grave, where the grass has now grown over the dirt.

We are ready for spring; we are ready for new life.

Today, we are going home from our grief pilgrimage

through Asia.

"We go back to rebuild," Andrew whispers to me as we stand in line to board the plane.

We talk about "trying again." It feels wrong, and it feels right. We are orphaned parents in need of a child. Will we have the courage try again? I don't know. I am scared to be hopeful. Yet I can't help but be hopeful.

I can see the sun cresting the skyline as our plane rises with it. Our transatlantic flight over the next thirty-six hours will allow us to live today twice— to see two sunrises and two sunsets within the same day. Is it coincidence that the autumnal equinox is today? Is it a day to stop and breathe before we tilt toward a new season?

As I watch the sun rise and set each time today,
I think about my little boy somewhere with God, splashing hues of pink and orange across the sky. If I listen closely, I can hear Brave yelling, with every bucket of sunset he throws,

"Momma, Daddy, come! This way, toward the sun!"

And so, we tilt. Closer to our beautiful brave new season.

-Christy

*E*leven months after your birth...

The wet, overgrown grass next to your grave is uncomfortable to settle in. No other child has been buried right next to you, which sends both comfort and jealousy through me. It's hard to explain the way our grief has evolved over time. The waves of physical heartache have begun to subside, and we are moving into a more peaceful place, grateful that the heavy sadness has eased.

Still, there is tension between how to become the first bloom after a forest fire, without abandoning you. The process of excavating hope has been arduous. But miraculously, we are sprouting green leaves.

"We just need to experience more life than death," your aunt said, as we walked out of my prenatal appointment.

It won't be long before we meet your little brother. I feel him moving inside of me, full of life, yet anxiety still shadows me wherever I go. How could I not be afraid?

But my little sister's words bring some relief.
My body has carried death. Now it carries life.
And living things need to experience more life than death, until fear of death fades beneath new blooms faithfully tended.

We will be brave enough to name that we have been marked by death, while being assured by you, Brave son, that death has not won. We will listen to you shout it from the sky, "He is risen!"

So, what will I be known for as your mother?
What will my name bring to mind when our loss of you comes up in conversation?

Will an image of my ravaged face, contorted with grief, come to mind… or will it be a picture of victory, of life, of wonder at the mystery of it all?

The more I learn of who you are, I know you as the son of bravery, the grandson of light.

I will not disgrace your life by lying in the grave. I will welcome the resurrection.

I will attempt to birth new life, try again to grow a family. Although naiveté is gone, my wild and free spirit will laugh, dance, and play.

I will not be found idle with kindness or stingy with love, for there are too many hurting people who have survived loss and need to be reminded that they are not alone.

I will be brave enough to speak truth to darkness, life to death, and hope to fear.

I love you, son.

-Your Momma

Made in the USA
Lexington, KY
23 December 2018